PAINED

on

PURPOSE

LOLITA A. BAKER

ISBN 979-8-88751-375-1 (paperback)
ISBN 979-8-88751-376-8 (digital)

Christian Faith Publishing
832 Park Avenue
Meadville, PA 16335
www.christianfaithpublishing.com

Printed in the United States of America

The day my life shifted from being born into this world to being traumatized physically, mentally, and emotionally. I know the Bible says we are born in sin and shaped in inequity, but not in a million years as a child did I see what was about to happen to me. The amazing thing about life is we don't remember everything, but we do have moments we never forget. The only good memory, before what I am about to share with you happened, that I can recall as a child was me joking and having fun with my abuser's family and my mom. I don't remember my exact age on that day, but I was a little child, and I immediately remember everyone laughing at me for being silly. I had such a big smile on my face because I was happy inside and out. Let me do a little rundown. My abuser was a stepdad of mine who is now deceased.

My mom married three times in her lifetime before she passed away. I don't remember much from her first marriage because I was too young. She was married to my brother's dad (who is also deceased). I only remember the things she shared with me and a few highlighted moments from that marriage. The second marriage was the one of my abuse, which I am about to share. The third one, I must admit, is the reason I still believe in love, family, and so much more because he was the total opposite of what I went through with the abuser. He was the stepdad who cared, and it showed. Not saying he was perfect, but he was the kind of stepdad that worked hard, provided, and made time to do little things like cook. I know how to make homemade gravy because he stood by the stove and showed me how to do it.

When mom was working, he did things like that when he got off work and so much more, and he never tried any of those horrible things that I had done to me by the abuser, and I admired him so very much for that. But he is also deceased. He passed away two years before my mom did. As you are reading this, you may be asking yourself about my biological dad, but I only have a few highlighted moments with him. He wasn't a part of my life. I may have seen him four or five times in my whole life. He was never mean or anything toward me. He just wasn't a part of my life. My mom told me the last time she took me to see him and before she passed away to do all I can to always stay in contact with him, and I did. I even reached out by phone when she passed away to tell him of her passing. His words to me were, "I won't be able to make it."

I never asked him to come. I just called to let him know that my mom passed away. And every phone call after that, I never got an answer until it finally said the phone is no longer in service. I honestly don't know if he is dead or alive, but I have prayed about that whole situation and given it all over to *God*. I have never hated or felt anything bad toward my dad, and I don't know all of him or my mom's past, but my mom was always one who wanted to do the right thing, not saying that she always got it all right, but that was something I learned from her. Even when she got things wrong, she would do all she could to try to make it right, or I would hear her praying about it. Sometimes she would ask me what I thought about certain situations. Even before passing, she confessed some things to me that I still think about to this day. Words are so powerful, and I am so glad for every word she spoke to me.

Now fast-forwarding to when it all started, my mom and my abuser (stepdad) both worked, and when she worked, he was with us whenever he wasn't working. I must warn you that some details I am about to share can be heart-wrenching. The day it started, I was six years old. So he did some welding and other things at that time, but he took me to work with him that day. I had no idea my life was about to change in a major way. I was sitting on the passenger side of his vehicle. I don't even remember what he said right before he touched me, but he put his hands on my legs and began to rub me in a very uncomfortable way, and I was so scared, then he started to touch my private area. I had on a dress that day, and he started saying nasty things I never heard before, then he unzipped his pants and told me to touch his private area, and then he said, "Put your mouth here."

I was extremely scared and confused. I didn't know what to do. There was no warning for me, and nobody ever told me anything about this type of behavior, but I somehow knew that something was wrong with it all. So then he picked me up and told me to sit down in his private area and proceeded to try and finish whatever he had planned to do to me. I was devastated, shaking, and crying tremendously and even more after it was done. I remember sitting on that same passenger's side, shaking like a very cold person, and he opened the glove compartment of his vehicle and pulled out this gun. I started to shake even harder like someone having a seizure. I didn't know what he was about to do. He took the gun out and put it on my leg and said to me, "If you say anything, I will blow your mom and your brother's brains out."

I was so super scared. I can't even remember how the rest of that day went because I was in some type of shock. It was like I died at that very moment, except I was still breathing. I immediately took on the spirit of fear. I was sad and very low in spirit and so much more that I will share throughout this book.

Now all of this that I've shared so far took place up until I was the age of twelve. This was only the beginning of so many other things to come. He then started to have fights with my mother. He abused her physically and verbally. He would do and say so many horrible things to her. He didn't like my brother at all. He showed it in his actions toward him. We would overhear them (my abuser and my mom) fighting and screaming at each other a lot. It was not a home of peace at all, and there was little ole me holding inside so much that I couldn't even share because of fear. I tried to stay far away from him. I tried to hide the same way I hid my feelings and what he had done to me. Whenever he was around, even with me and my cousins, I distanced myself. None of them knew why I was being so quiet and so distant. Might I add, my mom was a minister, but it never stopped him from doing things to her and to me. He got worse by the day.

I felt, as a child, very low. It felt like everywhere I went, I was being hurt, abused, talked about, and attacked. I'm about to share a situation that I often share a lot, especially when I'm teaching the youth, and sometimes I share it when I'm led, even with adults. It was a painful time for me as well. I was in third grade, and there was this boy in my class who picked on me every day. He talked about my cloth's and shoes and called me names and all. I remember feeling so sad every day at school. For about three months, I was being bullied. If you have never been bullied before, I will tell you it is just as painful as that sexual abuse was to me, not to mention I was still dealing with that on top of this now. So just as I was taught by my abuser, I tried to hide the pain, and in doing this, it caused depression.

There are different kinds of depression. But to just describe it, by definition, depression is a common and serious medical illness that negatively affects how you feel, the way you think, and how you act. Unfortunately, it is sadness and/or a loss of interest in activities you once enjoyed. So I went on hiding this extra pain. So I thought I was hiding it.

One day, my mom noticed my sadness, and she noticed me not wanting to eat. I remember sitting on the sofa after school so sad, and she looked at me and said, "Lolita, what's wrong with you?"

This wasn't like sexual abuse. I didn't feel the pressure when I couldn't speak, so I told her immediately. I said, "This boy picks on me every day," and I told her all the things he said.

She told me first to pray for him, and then she said, "Ignore him."

In both, I didn't know how to do either; and being a child, I said out loud to her, "PRAY." With a childlike mind, I did not want to pray for him, but I did because my mom told me to, and I honestly believed she prayed also because she was a woman of prayer. So I went to my room, and I was asking God to make him leave me alone. I didn't know what else to say.

Mom told me to also ignore him, and when I said I don't know how, she said, "Think about something else, something that you like," and I tried it. I can say that it actually worked. I still do it to this day, but I'm very skilled at it now. I can be standing right in front of someone talking and not hear a thing they are saying. I guess that was good quality as long as I am ignoring what I need to, it has saved me a lot of arguments and disagreements, but it also caused some as well when in relationships. I've learned that communication is very important. After all that, I went on to school and, to my surprise, this day would be different. When I got to class, I sat at my desk as usual, and there was an announcement over the school intercom. They asked for donations, that if anyone had anything to give— food, clothes, everyday necessities, anything to give to this family who lost everything in a house fire, and then they said his name—the one who bullied me.

I immediately turned my head and looked at his desk, and he wasn't there. I couldn't wait to get home and tell Mom all that happened. I came home, saying, "Mom! Mom!" with excitement on my face. I was just glad he wouldn't be able to pick on me anymore. But after I told her everything, being the woman of God that she was, she said, "Lolita, go into the kitchen cabinet and get some canned foods and give it to them."

I was like, "What? But he has been mean to me."

She said, "Go get the food."

So I did, and I remember grabbing from the few things we had, some canned food, and I put it in a grocery bag. The next day, I got to school, and when I got to the class, he was the first person I saw, and I walked up to him and gave it to him. He looked at me with this strange kind of confused look, and then he hugged me so tight. He had never done anything like that before, and then he said, "Thank you."

From that day forward, he never bullied me ever again. There were a lot of lessons taught here for him and for me. Mom was teaching me how to do the Word of God without me even knowing it. In Luke 6:27–28, Jesus said, "But I say unto you which hear, Love your enemies, do good to them which hate you, and pray for them which despitefully use you." I learned to pray to God, and I also learned a lesson on how to love. In this case, love and kindness broke the yoke of bondage off of me. I can't speak for him on what he learned, but his actions showed so much appreciation and gratitude toward me, and he didn't just appreciate what I gave him, but he stopped doing what he was doing to me, and that was awesome to me. I don't know what led him to start bullying me. I didn't bother anyone. I was too sad to even think of bothering anyone in third grade, but I learned a lot from the whole situation that I continue to share even now. I pray that God will continue to allow me to share it with many others, especially youth. Now in continuing on with all that my abuser did to me.

I have some memories of certain times he tried me over the years before he died. We were going to Franklinton, Louisiana, where some of my abuser's family lived to have fun in the summer, swimming and so much more. It was supposed to be an enjoyable day but, for me, it wasn't. My cousins and all came. Everyone was so excited to go and, somehow, he had all of us with him. The night came, and he got a hotel room. I don't even know how he ended up with us, but I was trying to stay far away from him. So he got this room with double beds, and my cousins were laughing and enjoying themselves, talking about all the fun they had that day. Then his voice spoke. I looked up at him. His eyes were red. They always looked red for some reason, and he said, "Lolita, come sit by me."

And I shook my head and said no.

So then he put his hand on the bed, lightly hitting it (tapping), and said, "Come over here" with a very deceptive tone of voice and smile on his face. I still said no with my head down and got closer to my cousins in fear. He then pulled out all this money and laid it on the bed and asked again. Might I add, I'm a little girl, so I was even more confused. But I later found out he had another problem and, for a long time, I wondered why was he trying to give me money and buy me expensive things. So I still said no and that I wouldn't go.

And I could hear my cousins saying, "Look at that money. You are crazy. I would take it. I would go."

But I remained quiet, and I stayed away from him. I knew he was going to try and touch me or something. I am sharing moments I remember of the abuse.

There was another time that I remember that revealed why he acted in the way he did. So this particular day, he took me to our capital city, Jackson, Mississippi, in which we also lived several times. But he took me to an adult store. Me still a child, not knowing what it was, he pulled up and asked me if I wanted anything out of it. I said no.

He said, "That's okay. I'm going to get you something."

And I was in the car the whole time. For one, I was too young to even be there. My mom was working. She had no idea, and he never took my brother anywhere that I can remember. He was in there for some time, then he came back to the car with a bag in hand and pulled out this object I had never seen before. As I got older, I knew what it was. But at that age, I didn't even know what it was, but it was an adult toy. He said out of his mouth, "This is for you. I'm going to use this on you," and he turned it on. I was so scared all over again.

This next particular time, he took me to this house where prostitutes were. I didn't know what that was then, but it all made sense later, and people kept going in and out of the house the whole time while I was sitting in the car. He went inside. He was in there for a very long time also, and I remember looking out the window, wondering when he was going to come out. Finally, he came out, and this woman came with him, and she got in the car also. He asked me to get in the back seat, so I did, and she pulled out this roll of condoms. Me being a child, I didn't know what that was then, but I could describe what they looked like.

He never worried about me saying anything because he knew I was scared from the very first time he put that gun on my leg, so it didn't bother him to do things like this. I was so lost and couldn't talk to anyone about how I felt and what I was going through as well as all I was seeing. I also remember him and Mom separating, and I was so happy inside, saying to myself, "Yes, it is finally about to be over, and he wouldn't bother me anymore (so I thought)." I know I have shared a lot already from the youngest age that I can remember up until age twelve, but before I even start on the next phase of my life, I must say, to all who read this and are going through or have been through some of these things that I have mentioned so far or even similar situations, *God* kept you here for a reason.

Sometimes it's hard to understand the why beneath the why it is all happening or has happened the way it did, but the more you walk with *God*, the more you will know why. And although it seems like nothing is going right or working for you in your life, don't believe the voice of the enemy that speaks negative thoughts to your mind but know that *God* has a purpose for it all. Jeremiah 29:11 says it like this, "For I know the thoughts that I think toward you, saith the Lord, thoughts of peace, and not of evil, to give you an expected end." Ecclesiastes 7:8 also says, "Better is the end of a thing than the beginning thereof: and the patient in spirit is better than the proud in spirit."

And this next scripture I hold dear to my heart simply because I was going through some of my mom's things after she passed away and found this scripture written on a piece of paper in her handwriting. It was always easy to tell her handwriting because she was left-handed and, for some reason, she slanted everything she wrote down in one direction, and that is Isaiah 55:8, and it says, "For my thoughts are not your thoughts, neither are your ways my ways, saith the Lord." Life is so amazing in many ways, even when we have bad experiences. And although all of our stories and the things we go through may be different, *God* remains the same—he still heals, he still saves, he still delivers, he still sets the captive free, he still reigns, and he knows all things. Yes, he could stop a lot of things, but when he doesn't, we must continue to trust him and have faith in his plans for our lives.

Job said it best in Job 13:15. He said, "Though he slay me, yet will I trust in him: But I will maintain mine own ways before him."

Now it is time to journey from the ages of thirteen to age eighteen, the adolescent years. Thirteen, while doing some research on the number thirteen, I was surprised by what I found. I found out that it symbolizes death, but it also symbolizes rebirth to the spirit and is a symbol of new life. Now I for one don't get caught up in everything I see, hear, or read, but when God makes things as clear as this, I can only believe.

At age thirteen, my abuser died. It was also the same year I gave my life to Christ. This is so powerful in so many ways because I didn't know what I was doing, but my mom kept taking me to church with her. It seemed like every time she went, she said, "Lolita, get washed up, and let's go to church."

The age that I can remember when God first touched me was age nine. I was in a church service with my mom. She often traveled a lot as an evangelist, so I witnessed and saw a lot at a young age, but it was a revival that a friend of hers was preaching at, and I remember her making me get in this prayer line, and I was so nervous because people were falling out on the floor after she touched them, and I had never seen anything like that before. So when I got to the preacher, she said, "God is going to touch you tonight."

And I was so scared. She said, "Lift your hands."

And I did, and she began to pray. And when she prayed and touched me, all I remember was feeling this strong supernatural touch, not from her hands, although she touched me. It was stronger and it was so different and so powerful that I went out into the spirit, and I was on the floor, and I remember these people helping me get up, and when I got to my seat, I kept thinking about that touch that I felt. It was my first personal encounter with the Holy Spirit.

This next time, being thirteen years old, I was in a service with my mom, listening to another preacher talk about God and who he is and how he wants to save you from all your troubles. And I was sitting there, thinking I want all my troubles to go away, and he sounds like the one who can take it away. So, at age thirteen, I basically ran to the altar to be saved. Nobody knew all I had been through or what I was still dealing with, the hidden things, but I was ready to let it all go. So I gave my life to God. My mom didn't force me or anything. I just heard the preacher and wanted a change.

When it was all over, I thought my troubles were about to be over, but little did I know, there was more to come. This is why I am like I am now. The first thing I tell others is that it won't always be easy, but God will see you through every trial and tribulation. During those times when he and Mom separated, we went through so much. We grew up very poor and, at one time, we didn't have a place to live. My abuser had purchased a house for us when they were together, but when they separated, she lost the house. One of her friends let us stay over until she was able to find something. One of her sisters gave her an old house. It was so hard living there. When I lay down at night, I looked up and saw the sky, and when we walked on the floor, I remember seeing the ground. And living in the middle of the country, I remember rats falling down on the bed from the open roof. I had my head covered. I was so scared, and I was lying under my mom all the time. She was trying so hard to raise us by herself. I saw her not eating food just so we could eat.

Lights would be out, and she would light candles. I remember asking her, "Mom, do you want some of my food?"

But she wouldn't take it. Those were trying times for her, and even though I didn't see her cry during those times, as a mom, I know it hurt her. She had such a great desire to finish college. She wanted to be a cosmetologist (and oftentimes she used me as her living mannequin), but every time she went, something happened, and she never finished. I remember her pushing me in a grocery cart to the grocery store in our capital city. Gosh, there were so many hard times that I thanked God and her for later in life. She told me things concerning her past when I got older, about her and her siblings being taken out of school and so much more, and she even experienced rape at a young age. So my mom went through a lot as well that I found out about later from her.

But still being thirteen, one day, while sleeping in the living room, my brother was in his room, and there was an entrance through the front door. I heard my mom's voice, and she said, "Look who is here?"

And when I looked up, I saw him again (my abuser). She didn't know all I had been through, and I just assumed they had some type of conversation and tried to work things out between them. But all types of emotions, along with other things, were rushing through my brain and heart, and I felt sadness, instantly, all over again. I don't remember exactly what day of this same year, but it was after he came back into the picture. Mom told me he had a brain tumor (cancer). But I was starting to have inner anger problems, and it felt like I didn't have any feelings whatsoever when it came down to him. I was a broken child. So, when she said it, it didn't mean anything to me at all.

This one particular day, after finding out about the cancer, we were at one of my aunt's houses. He was still able to drive at this point, but this was the final time he tried to make his last move. He called me to his vehicle. I went up to the door, and he tried me sexually for the last time. I remember walking away so angry, thinking to myself, *You are sick and still trying to mess with me.* Then everything shifted for the worst for him after that last moment. He got sicker and sicker. I never understood why Mom took him back. There was a time I went to church with her, and we were there a very long time. Mom liked to talk with her church friends (lady friends) after church and, sometimes, those conversations lasted a very long time. I was with her, thinking, *Mom, can we go now?*

But when we got home, he was there, ready to fight her. It got so bad. This was the worst fight ever, and all this took place before she took him back. But it was so tragic that I just have to share it. He took the TV and threw it at Mom, and my brother was so upset, so my abuser and my brother started yelling at each other. I never heard my brother rage in such a way. I started screaming really loud so my brother took this cemented statue of a dog Mom had off the floor. It was big, and he threw it at him and knocked him out. He fell backward on the floor. I thought he was dead. I was screaming loud and crying, and Mom went into her room, very upset and packing her things while the police were on the way.

So much was going on all at one time, and for the very first time ever, my mom asked me a question while I was sitting on the bed. She asked me, "Has he ever touched you?"

And I looked up at her so fearfully, and I paused for a very long time, wanting to say yes, wanting to tell her everything, and then I remembered the gun and what he said he was going to do to her and my brother, and I dropped my head with a very sad look on my face and shook it and said no.

She was still enraged by the fight when she was talking. I remember her saying she dreamed about him messing with young girls and, there I was, I couldn't say a mumbling word because of fear. So the police came. He didn't die that very moment from that fight, but it was the cancer that took him out. During those times, he got very sick and was hospitalized. My mom was there for him every step of the way. They were still legally married, and this one day, she told me to come to the hospital with her. I didn't even want to go. I had so many inner things going on inside of me, but I went anyway. And when I saw him, it scared me. He had lost all his hair with only like three strands on his head. He couldn't talk. He didn't look like himself. He was very small.

After seeing all of that, it wasn't long after that he died. Then came the time for his funeral. It hurt my mom a lot, but I honestly didn't have one feeling. It was so weird.

One day after his passing, I went into my mom's restroom, and there was a picture of him hanging in the mirror. And all I remember thinking was I got to tell my mom, "Now he is dead, and he can't hurt anyone." But how was I going to do that? And how would she take it? So I went to one of my cousins, who had been through exactly what I was going through. We both were able to talk about what we had been through, so I asked her if she would come with me to tell my mom. It was a hard thing to do, but I had to let her know. And when I did, she immediately got upset. She wasn't mad at me, and not one time did she doubt me. She was asking me why I didn't say anything. She was very upset about him. It was like she wished he was alive to take it out on him, in so many words.

I remember she had flowers from the funeral in the house also. But when I told her about everything that he did to me, she threw them all away, then she ripped the picture of him up and tore it into pieces. Now that I'm older and hearing all of my family talk about my mom's past history of fighting before God saved her, I can't even imagine how all of that would have unfolded if she had known sooner. Would she even be alive? Would my brother be alive? Or would anyone be in jail? So many times, I asked how that may have unfolded, but everything happens for a reason, even when it's a tragedy.

After sharing all of that, I started living what was supposed to be a normal teenage life, but I never dealt with the things I had inside of me for all those years. Then I started to act out in school, at home, everywhere. At fourteen, I had my first encounter with a boy. This time, it wasn't me being forced to do anything, and I was headed down a very long dark road, not knowing which way to go. I got in my first relationship at age fifteen. I did so many things that were wrong, and I hardly cared about anything. People hurt me, and I also hurt people. I got worse and worse at being angry and everything you can name. People would say things to my mom like, "Look at your children. How are you going to preach to us? Look at how bad your children are."

And I know that had to have hurt her, but being in the position I'm in now in life, I know that, sometimes, these issues have to be addressed and handled properly or lots of other consequences will follow. But for me and my issues, I learned the hard way. And I had to deal with them as it was given to me, which has now, in my adult life, given me such a deep passion to help others.

So when the first guy I was with broke up with me, I didn't know how to handle the pain. I was fifteen years old. So I tried to take my own life. I took a lot of pills. I just wanted to die. It was way bigger than him breaking up with me. I was still hurting from my childhood pains. The good news in that situation is that God did not let me die. He just let me sleep. I must share my spiritual experiences. Even as a child, I always had these dreams that would come true, and then I would see things with my eyes open, and it often scared me. I was so afraid to sleep at night because I might see something. I remember sneaking into my brother's room at night and hiding under his bed so I wouldn't be in the room by myself seeing things. I remember dreaming of a couple of family members dying before they died, and I told my mom when I dreamt it, and then it happened. So I was scared to see anything else.

It happened so often that my mom would listen very closely every time I said, "Mom, I had a dream." She was my go-to person because I didn't understand what was going on with me. Not to mention I was being a bad teenager. I also knew that God was calling me. He made it very clear. I could tell from the things I dreamed and saw, and Mom would tell me more about what I wasn't supposed to do but, of course, I did the opposite. I was a very rebellious teenager. She kept taking me to church, but I was in there with a thousand thoughts running through my mind. Most of the time, I didn't even want to be there. I gave her such an attitude sometimes when she asked me to come. I didn't want to wear those dresses she made me wear or anything, and when she would ask me to get up and sing, I had my hands folded while doing it.

The only thing at that time I enjoyed doing at church was reading the Scriptures. For some reason, I always asked God to give me something to read, and I got excited, inside, whenever I would read them, not even knowing why. For many years, she took me everywhere she went, and I started asking her, "Why don't you make my brother go like you make me go?" as if I was grown or something.

Although I was acting out, I was really a nice person, and those mothers at church would say, "Your daughter has such a sweet spirit."

I didn't know what they meant by it, but for them to see anything good out of me being bad was shocking. In reality, I was acting out my inner pains. So I became a very sad teenager inside. I felt so low, and just when it couldn't get any worse, I started failing in school.

I remember failing a lot of grades, and my mom just wouldn't give up on me, so she sent me to summer schools until I passed the grades I failed. But what she didn't know and what my teachers didn't know was I had an inner battle, and they kept trying to figure out why I was failing. I will never forget this day. They called us to the school, and I walked into the office with them and my mom, and they told her I wasn't smart enough to be in the regular classes with the other children, and that they were putting me in a special education class. I was so upset that I got even angrier and stormed out of the office, saying all types of things. But I did what they asked, and I took the classes for about three months, then they called my mom back, and we had to go back to the office again. This time they said I am too smart for the special education classes. I felt so bad inside. I felt like I didn't belong anywhere, and they didn't even know.

I remember being in the classroom, especially when I was younger, and the teacher would be standing, teaching, and all I could hear was ringing in my ears. I was sitting, thinking about the abuse so much that I couldn't hear a thing she was saying in class. It was one of the reasons I failed a lot. Then I started feeling dumb, and there were times in the classroom I had sexual thoughts that came from what I had been through, which led to those types of behaviors. In sharing all of this, my prayer is that it will help somebody else who may be in this place to be free from all the pains and attachments that are associated with these types of traumas and that it will make parents and guardians aware of the things children go through also while digging deeper into why they are acting out and why they are feeling low.

It's not always things like what I went through, but it is always a why beneath the why. I must admit, even though I didn't want to go to church half the time, and I was doing the most, my mom bringing me to church taught me a lot. I didn't get what she desired for me at that time because I was so caught up in my own personal problems. I learned a lot that even when I was out with my teenage friends, I would always be the one encouraging them when they were going through something. Somehow I was telling them about God and what he could do. I wasn't living right at all, but I believed in God with my whole heart. I remember getting so mad this one time when this guy was saying there is no God, and he started saying all types of crazy things about God. I remember just going off on him.

Might I add, I wasn't living right. But something about that I did not like at all, and it triggered a different type of emotion in me. Just by reading this, you can tell I was a very lost child still growing in age and height and even weight, but that little child who was abused at six was still there, needing help. So I would go in and out, try to live right, and then try to do what I was seeing. One minute, I'd be at church; next, I would be out, doing things that I knew were wrong.

I remember being on my knees, one time, singing to God, telling him how much I love him. I was so broken, but I wanted him to know that I love him. In all of the things I have been through, I never got angry at God, but I was very angry in my actions. Then I found something that I loved to do, and that was playing basketball.

It became such a joy for me. I used to say I was going to be a "dare to be different" teen, but that didn't happen.

At seventeen, I started experimenting with alcohol, and once, after a game, some of my peers were smoking marijuana, and when they kept asking me, I finally gave in. I didn't want to feel odd and left out, so I tried it for the first time. But my coach was a Christian, and he used to have us pray before games. Sometimes he would read the Word out of the Bible to us. He is a person I thank God for that helped pushed me to want to do better. I didn't do everything right, and I still don't always get it all right, but he is one of the reasons I graduated high school. Because I loved basketball, I had to have the grades to play; but even in basketball, I had bad behavior starting out. I even threw a towel at him during one game and stormed out, but him being the nice man that he was, he never ever did or said anything to me hurtful or out of the way, and I admired him for that.

He went the extra mile and drove us from basketball games and practices, and that meant a lot, especially coming from a single-parent home. He became a dad figure to me without even knowing it. He would get on to us about being out at all times of the night. This one time, I was out past the time he told us to be in. I had on all my basketball gear and shoes when he clearly told us not to be out or in our gear, and I saw him in the store. I ran behind some chips, trying to hide from him. That was so funny. He never said anything until we got to practice. He didn't mention my name, he just addressed the situation. He never used vulgar language, and it made me want to do better.

Everything about him pushed me to want to be better. There was a time I struggled in some classes, and one of my teammates tutored me after school. She was so amazing and a great teacher, and she never made me feel like I was dumb. She helped me pull a D all the way up to a B in a short period of time. I remember telling her, "You should be a teacher one day," not knowing what I was saying. Even today, she is a teacher, and she taught my two oldest children in school when they attended that school.

Speaking of children, I got pregnant at age eighteen, my senior year, and I became sad all over again. Now I couldn't play basketball.

Not knowing what I was going to do next, I couldn't take care of a child. I didn't even know where to start, but I had to tell my mom. She didn't hate me for it, but she sure did preach to me like never before. One particular morning, getting ready to go to school, I drove. My mom had bought me an old car, and I was going to pick my cousin up for school to ride with me, and when I got to her house, I went inside. I asked her if she was ready. She said she was coming. While standing there, blood began to flow from my body uncontrollably. I started screaming out, "I'm bleeding!" And I was so scared 'cause I didn't know what was going on with me, and it wouldn't stop.

Another one of my cousins was there, and she said, "You are probably having a miscarriage."

I was like, "What is that?" I had zero knowledge of any of these things.

She said, "You need to go to the doctor."

I was scared, but I went, and she was right. I was having a miscarriage. I didn't know how to feel. I cried so much, and then they called my mom and told her that I had to have surgery. That was a very painful and scary moment, and it took me a while to recover. I went back to school, and I remember wanting to play basketball again, but I didn't feel I would be able to, and I don't think my coach even knew how to ask me, but he sent a teammate, and she said he asked if I wanted to play again. I was so excited just because he asked. I was like, "Yes, yes, yes!" But I had moments where I got weak in practice. I would get so dizzy and so much more, but I got through it all by the grace of God. Might I add, my coach led us to the state championship in high school. When I tell you he coached a team who went from losing almost every game in junior high to winning more than losing in high school and made champions out of us, he was the best and worked us like crazy, but the hard work paid off.

We won the first round but didn't get the final round, so we got second place trophy. But it still felt super good, a moment I'm sure none of us will ever forget as a team altogether. I finally graduated, and I literally tell people today that me graduating from high school was nothing but a miracle. I learned something very special during those years, and that is God will put the right people in our lives to help pull us through any situation no matter how tough the situation may be. And I'm grateful for each and every person he has sent along the way to help push me to be better. It is amazing how something so small as our childhood can be a foundation that shapes our whole future. Who I became at that age was a reflection of what I had been through, like a diamond in the rough, needing to learn so much to be able to grow into who I was created to be. But it was still only the surface of what is to come.

At this point in life, I was growing up and had to live with the choices I made for myself, and all my choices weren't always good. Some things I went through were because of the choices I made. I learned that the hard way also and am still learning, even today, that every choice, whether good or bad, has consequences. I don't write this as a victim because I am not a victim anymore. *I am victorious* because of *Christ Jesus* who saved me. And although I had many bad things done to me, I also did so much wrong in my lifetime that if I had written it years ago when I was asked to write a book, it would have probably been written from a hurtful place because I wasn't healed, and I hadn't forgiven myself and others.

God placed a friend in my life that mentioned this to me before I didn't even know that I needed to forgive myself also. After my abuser died, I had this dream, and he appeared in it. He didn't look sad at all. He was smiling like a free person, but when I saw him in the dream, I remember yelling in a loud voice, "Why did you do this to me? Why, why, why?" And he stopped smiling, dropped his head, and walked away, and I woke up. That was an eye-opening dream for me. I was still angry at him, and he was dead and gone. I needed to forgive him for my own freedom. It is so amazing how God shows us ourselves when we need it the most. He was no longer alive, so I couldn't go to him, but I prayed for God to help me to let it go. I remember saying, "Lord, I forgive him." And it may sound like small words, but it was a freedom card for me. I no longer felt trapped inside.

Forgiveness is so powerful, and when you have truly forgiven someone, you will feel that inner peace even when whoever wronged you comes around. Although with him it was a dream, I've had many other experiences that taught me this lesson. But I did not know how to forgive until I started learning about it in church and through the Word of God. In Matthew 6:14–15, Jesus said, "For if ye forgive men their trespasses, your heavenly Father will also forgive you: but if ye forgive not men their trespasses, neither will your Father forgive your trespasses."

It is not always easy. This is why we pray and ask God to help us to forgive. I've learned that with the help of the Holy Spirit, we can conquer anything, for there is nothing too hard for him. Sometimes it takes longer, the process of breaking the layers, because forgiveness has four major stages: first, you have to uncover the anger; second, you have to decide to forgive; then you have to work on forgiveness so that you can then be released from the emotional prison that unforgiveness puts us in when we choose not to forgive. This is something we must master in life because the enemy will continually try us in this area to hold us hostage in a prison with bars, and each bar represents unforgiveness toward somebody, and the only way to get out is to forgive. Nobody can set us free. We have to choose this freedom on our own.

The Word of God also taught me that no matter how many times the same person wrongs us, we still have to forgive them. In the book of Matthew 18:21–22, the Bible says, "Then came Peter to him, and said, Lord, how often shall my brother sin against me, and I forgive him? Till seven times? Jesus said unto him, I say not unto thee, until seven times: but, until seventy times seven." When Jesus said this, he wasn't giving an exact number, but he was indicating that we should be willing to forgive an indefinite number of times. He was making a point to forgive continuously. Now before I shift into adulthood, I must share experiences I had in that transition after high school.

My mom told me I had to go to college. I didn't have a clue of what I wanted to do in life, so I didn't even have a desire to go, but I went 'cause she was not going to let me stay home doing nothing. She saw how I did my hair so well and wanted me to have my own business, so she told me to take what she always wanted to do, and that was cosmetology. Although I could do it, I didn't have a desire for it, and where there is no desire, there is zero drive. I did very well in college, and I almost finished, but I had a made-up mind that I wasn't going back to school once it ended. And I ended up working in a factory for five years and still didn't quite know what I wanted to do. But it came to me later in life, and it happened in a unique way that I will share as I shift from my teenage years to my adult years.

The college years. My, my, my, where do I start? Even though I did good in classwork, there were many other things that happened in college. This time, Mom wasn't there. As a matter of fact, I went to college four hours away from home, and nobody was there that I knew. My roommate ended up getting pregnant before school actually started and didn't come, so I had this big room to myself also for about a week or so. I was all by myself until this one particular day, I went to the cafeteria to eat. I sat at this table by myself, and this girl there came to me and asked if I wanted to eat with her and her friends. So I said yes, and I went to eat with them. She was so nice to me, even though she was involved in some things like smoking marijuana and so on. She always treated me nice, but the more I hung out with her, the more I started to do what she did. I also had two friends that stayed in my dorm, one across from me and the other next door to me. The three of us became closer than I did with the friend who asked me to sit with her in the cafeteria.

College—I always call it my super crazy years. And it wasn't just me. One night, we had a block party. I remember going outside my dorm, and it was something I had never seen before. Everyone was drunk, high, sluggish, and so much more. When I share this story, I tell people it looked like Sin City to me. Not normal at all. But as teenagers, it was fun. So as I began to explore all the different things at school, somehow or another, I ended up joining the school choir. Oh my goodness, it was an amazing experience. We went to different places, singing and to other colleges, juvenile places, and so much more. We even participated in some choir competitions and traveled to churches. I can say choir saved me from where I was headed. None of my friends were in the choir, but the two that stayed by me in the dorm always came to support me. We always supported each other with all that we were going through.

As we were performing, one day, singing in a gospel concert, the Spirit of God fell so heavy on us. We were praising God on the stage. It was an outpouring experience. Our choir director was from Jamaica, and he was so talented with music. It was a tug-of-war going on in college, between good and evil. Both were present, and we had our own choices. So we often did both, which led to a lot of things not working. I remember, one day, the friend who first asked me to eat with them got into a serious fight. She was originally from Chicago and taking nursing classes. Everyone came to my room, saying she was in a fight. I was like, "What?"

They said, "Yes, a bad fight," in which the one she fought ended up in the hospital. It was so sad because she was such a nice person, and she had her plans all mapped out, but she got kicked out of school. I lost contact with her. I don't know if she had to do jail time or anything. But I learned a lot in college, just like I did in elementary and high school. Life is filled with so many learning experiences. It's not always about the bad but what we learn from the bad and apply to our lives that grow us into better people. In other words, we will always be learning till the day we die, in some way or another. College, for me, helped me deal with some of the insecurities I had. I remember having no confidence whatsoever because of what they did to me in high school, so when I approached my teacher in college with good grades and all, because I lacked confidence, I told her I wanted to quit.

She took me to her office, sat me down, and said, "Why do you want to quit?"

I said, "Because I can't do this like the other ladies do it." They didn't even have to try certain things, but I had to struggle with it, then I got it. But she said something to me that I will never forget.

She said, "I enjoy teaching you more."

I looked at her with a shocked look.

She said, "Yes, with someone like you, I get to teach you from scratch. And you are willing to learn." She said with them, they had their own way of doing things, which was harder to deprogram out of them.

You see, the way she was teaching us was setting us up to pass state boards, and it had to be done in a certain way. So although they were very good at what they did, it still had to be done correctly. My lesson in what my teacher told me was if you are willing to learn, you can do anything. She gave me a boost of confidence at that very moment. I also learned that we all do things differently. That doesn't make us less capable. We are unique in our own way, just as God has created us to be. My college years were filled with good times, bad times, and even trying times, but I learned a lot from every experience.

To everyone reading this and especially the young people who are facing all kinds of hardships, college can bring out the best in you as well as the worst. It's all about choice and decisions. Remain focused on what you have set in your heart to do and, each day, let God help you get through every challenge. With him, all things are possible. Sometimes he changes our plans to fit his plan, and when we allow him to have his way and just go with the flow, it will speak later that his plan worked together for our good. Romans 8:28 says it like this, "And we know that all things work together for good to them that love God, to them who are the called according to his purpose." Glory to God.

As I now enter into the stages of my adulthood, I must start by saying that this part of my life is still being written, but I will share some moments from age twenty-one up until now, as I feel led by *God* to help somebody else reading this even now, and some things I know will have to be written later in future books to come. So I will just start here.

The first major moment for me was getting pregnant again. In sharing all of these adult moments, it's not to intentionally hurt or bring shame to anyone involved. I thank God for the new mindset and the freedom after all of these life-changing moments. This is why I mention my own faults and wrongs as well while sharing every testimony because there are many things in life that I have done to others also, and many things that I have gotten wrong.

With that being known, I will say at age twenty-one, I met my oldest child's dad. Of course I was young. He was much older than me. And to be honest, at this stage in my life, I thought I was grown. As the older generation would say it, a know-it-all. I thought I knew how to handle life, so I was just out there in the world, learning most things the hard way. Even though I was out there doing the most, there were certain things I vowed never to do. But because of my immaturity, this whole experience was one I was not ready for at all. I met my oldest child's dad who was much older than me, and we were still getting to know one another. This relationship lasted over a period of two and a half years. We slept together very soon, and I got pregnant quickly, and I was partying and drinking. That was not really a thing he liked to do, but it was what I did to have fun. We also worked together during that time.

But the way I found out I was pregnant, I know now that it was definitely the hand of God protecting my unborn child from all the things I was doing during that time. I wanted to miss work this particular day, so I told myself and a friend of mine at the time that I will just go to the local clinic to get a checkup just to get a doctor's excuse for work. Might I add, I didn't miss a period for that month or anything, so I was clueless. I remember going there and getting everything done, and then this nurse walks into the room and asked me, "Have you taken a pregnancy test at home?"

There I was, still naive and clueless about what she was trying to let me know. I said to her, "No, ma'am."

She then looked at me and said, "Well, ma'am, you are pregnant."

My eyes got so big like, how? As if I didn't know how, but I was still in total shock because in my mind, I was like, *I didn't come here for that*.

She showed me the evidence, and I said to her, "I have not even missed a period yet, and it was normal the month before."

Then she told me I was only three weeks.

I didn't even know you could find out that early, but it was the hand of God protecting the baby from everything that I was doing because as soon as I found out, I stopped drinking and everything that I knew could harm the unborn child. The time came now for me to tell her dad. He was shocked also but okay as well. So I began to go through my first full-term pregnancy, and there were good days and not-so-good days. I was very sick for the first three to four months and lost a lot of weight but eventually started feeling better and regained my appetite and strength to carry her. But something devastating happened that I was not ready for. I was six months pregnant when this happened. This particular day, we were at work, and I had just come off my lunch break. And when I got back to my work area, this lady came up to me and spoke words I was not ready for at all. She said, "You know he's married, right?"

And I said, "Who?"

She was talking about my unborn child's father and, immediately, the pain in my heart dropped down to my stomach in such a major way for many reasons. I became angry all over again. Not to mention, in all of my wrongdoings, this was one of those things I would never, in my life, do. So I was very hurt and upset, and I even felt a strong feeling of betrayal, but I wanted to hear what he had to say. So when I saw him, I asked him about it and told him what she said to me. His response was, "She didn't even give me time to tell you."

And I got even angrier. I remember getting in my vehicle, one night, riding down the highway, saying to God, "I'm so sorry" with tears flowing from my eyes. I couldn't take the pain, so I pulled the vehicle over, and I began to weep, and I cried out so loud. Then I put my hands on my belly, and I kept asking God to forgive me. And I asked him to not let anything I went through happen to my child. I asked him to make her smart and not to ever allow her to go through what I went through in school and as a child. As I was still crying out with such a loud cry, I also asked him not to let what I had done affect her. And after I got it all out, I just cried until I couldn't cry anymore.

At this time in my life, I was so spiritually lost that I was missing the big picture of what God was trying to get me to see. Romans 6:23 says, "For the wages of sin is death; but the gift of God is eternal life through Christ Jesus our Lord." Since I was so spiritually blind, I tried to figure things out in my life on my own, which is the number one way to self-destruct.

Months later, we talked about everything, and he told me the whole situation, how they had separated, and that they ended everything, and he gave her this truck back and put the ring inside. And he also told me how her religion didn't believe in divorce. I never met this lady a day in my life, neither have we ever had any conversations out of the whole two-plus years we were together. And although they were done with one another, I knew, in my mind, we would never have what God intended if we did stay together with him still being legally married. So as time went on, I started to be very disrespectful toward him and very resentful and so much more after I had my daughter.

When I had her, it was one of the longest and hardest deliveries ever for me. That morning, I woke up okay, but later in the day, I got hungry and decided to drive to get something to eat, and I was in so much pain. I got back home. Her dad was getting ready for work, and the pain increased, and it hit me frequently. I was having contractions, and we knew she was on the way, so he drove me to the hospital, and I couldn't even talk because of all the pain I was in.

When we got inside the hospital, the nurse looked at me and said, "She is about to have this baby."

I was rushed to labor and delivery, and it was hard for her to come, so they called extra help into the room to try and help with delivering her. My mom was outside the room. She couldn't bear seeing me in all that pain and, finally, with all the extra help, her dad was there as well, she came into this world strong and healthy. I remember looking to see if she had all of her fingers and toes because I knew I messed up while carrying her early on, but it was a life-changing moment yet joyful, simply because she was alive and well. Other family members came to the hospital. It was something I never experienced in my life before, of course. But as time went on, I and her dad tried to stay together. And just to point the finger at myself, I honestly was not a good person to be with at this time. I was still dealing with childhood issues, and now, this new situation with him would only make matters worse. And I just stopped caring altogether, and it showed.

He was always a good dad to her and still is, and outside of all that we had going on, he is a very good person, even to this day. We had many other experiences, but these are the ones I feel led to share for now. I know that they will help somebody reading this. I always knew in the back of my mind that he was married, so I started to do things, which eventually led to us both ending it for good. After all of that, I remember saying to God, "I will not have another child until I am married," and I was very serious when I said it, and that's exactly what I did. I was still young and immature and basically a baby living in a grown woman's body because I was lost, broken, and unhealed. There is almost nothing that could be done that was wrong in the sight of God that I didn't do. I am one who can admit I was like the Apostle Paul said (a chief sinner), and I am not ashamed to admit it now.

So for a very long time, I was running from God. But I always knew that there was something different happening in my life when it came down to God because he always showed me things, even when I didn't understand them. I always knew it was him. I will never forget, before getting married, I was working in a factory, the one I was at for five years after college. And I had a dream in which I saw myself falling off this real high stand that I stood on at work, and it was a very long fall in the dream. It felt like I was about to die, but I landed on this big thing of cotton. It looked like clouds. Thinking about it now brings tears to my eyes because even though I didn't know what it meant when he showed it to me then, he later revealed it to me after I hit rock bottom later in life. He saved me, and that's what my landing on the cotton represented in the dream. He was showing me then that I would fall and that it was going to be long and hard and it was going to feel like I was going to die.

And soon after I had this dream, I reunited with a friend of mine who later asked me to marry him. I was twenty-six years old when I got married. He was in the military, and I was still working at the factory. When we married, I moved to California with him along with my daughter who was four years old at this time. Coming into our marriage, I already had come into it wrong. I want to help somebody reading this who may be dating right now. I often hear and heard many people say you are single until you are married and, legally, you are. But sometimes, the relationships you are in can be a hindrance to your next relationship if things aren't done in decency and in order. So when dating, pray and ask God for wisdom in what to do and how to do it, and also ask him to give you the strength to do it.

I sure wish I knew how to do that before getting married and so many more things I now know that I didn't know then. But we didn't, so it caused problems early on for us. When it comes to marriage, this will definitely be written in a different book in the future as I am led by God. But I will share different situations as I feel led spiritually also to help somebody reading this right now. Might I add, because of growth and forgiveness, I am able to talk to everyone that I have mentioned so far that is still alive. As God has grown me, I was even able to go back to some of them and share things God revealed to me, over time, including my ex-husband.

God saved me after my divorce. Or maybe I should say it like this: he drove me back to him into the kingdom of God because he had already saved me at age thirteen. One of the things God revealed to me as I began to grow and he opened my spiritual eyes is that we were both wrong. For many years, I blamed him for everything that went wrong. In reality, we were both wrong for a lot of reasons, but the main reason, I must admit, is spiritual. You may be wondering why I'm saying this. Well, once God brought me back into the kingdom of God, he put me under such a great leader whom he called to teach and preach the Gospel of Jesus Christ, and in which I will share more about that in this book also. But he taught me and many others the Word of God and the system of God. This is very important in life because it is written in Hosea 4:6 that we are destroyed for lack of knowledge, and I have found this to be very true in my life.

You see, my ex-husband and I didn't know the system of God, and neither did we live in it properly because we didn't know how, but we did, and we still do love God. But because we didn't know that we needed God and his Word to help guide us, we tried to figure things out on our own. We tried to work things out on our own, and we weren't living the life God wanted us to live. So it was easy for the enemy to get in and destroy things by doing what he does best and that is to cause division and confusion. And if God hadn't stepped in, it could have been killing because we were both spiritually blind. I didn't know how to pray for him. I can't speak for him, but I don't recall a time we ever prayed together either. And when I prayed, I was praying as I did as a child. I was asking God to make him leave me alone. I just didn't have the wisdom, knowledge, or understanding, and neither one of us knew what God required of us in our role as husband and wife. So, to sum it up, we were lost, trying to find our way.

I always knew God had something for me to do, though I just didn't know then what it was. As a matter of fact, I said to my ex-husband before we got married, not even knowing what I was saying, but it came out of my mouth. I said, "One day, God is going to use me for something." Then I asked him, "Will you be by my side?"

He looked at me and said yes.

And he was probably thinking, *What is she talking about?* Even when he left that night, I asked myself, "Why did you ask him that?"

Now before actually getting married, my mom had a talk with him. I wasn't in the room when they talked, but he came out sweating, and Mom said to me, "Don't get married." She never said why, she just said don't. She never forced me or anything, and she supported the decision we made together to do it anyway. You see, as a parent (me being one now), we know things. Not speaking for every situation, but some things we just know from our own experiences and so much more. But even in that, we still have choices to make in our own lives. And even though things didn't work out, I am forever thankful for every experience, whether good, bad, or ugly.

We didn't know anything about seeking God and getting his directions on even marrying before marriage. I just want to pause and encourage some teachers or anyone who have knowledge in these areas to keep on teaching and leading others as God leads you because you, opening your mouth, could save somebody else and keep them from going down a long dark road that God never intended for any of us to travel. We stayed married over a total of seven years, five of those years together and two of them separated before actually divorcing. I remember a time we tried so hard to make things work. We even sat down and wrote down things to try to work on, but it was like the enemy was right there, saying, "Not on my watch" 'cause everything we tried only got worse, and being spiritually lost, we didn't know how to handle it. But God blessed us with three wonderful children, and now I will share the experiences of each pregnancy and different testimonies of how God stepped in on all levels, each time.

My first son was born during a terrible storm (Hurricane Katrina). For some of you that may not know, Hurricane Katrina was a large and destructive Category 5 Atlantic hurricane that caused over 1,800 deaths and $125 billion in damage in late August 2005, especially in the city of New Orleans and the surrounding areas, with maximum sustained winds of 175 mph. The storm left millions homeless in New Orleans and along the Gulf Coast of Louisiana, Mississippi, and Alabama. I was in Mississippi at the time the storm made landfall. With my oldest son, I experienced gestational diabetes during pregnancy, something I never experienced before, along with other difficulties that I never experienced. Even when it came down to actually having him, the pain I experienced with my oldest daughter didn't even compare to the pain I experienced right before having him. With him, I was trying to just take the pain, and my doctor thought that it would take a while to have him, so he walked across the street to his office, which was across the street from the hospital.

My mom and my mother-in-law at that time were at the hospital, and my ex-husband even did the impossible and made it to the hospital from his military assignment with airports and all being closed because of the storm. He made it, but after trying to take the pain for so long, might I add, I couldn't do anything but cry. The doctor thought I would be pushing for some time like the hard time I had with my daughter, so he wasn't even in the room when my son came out. The nurses said, "Push" and then immediately screamed, "Stop."

He came out so fast that she almost dropped him. She was so super scared. It was all over her facial expressions. I didn't care. I was just glad he came out. But when the doctor walked in, he was so shocked. The nurse said to him, "I need to go home for the day," and they all laughed out loud. It was amazing how the more pain I had, the easier his birth became.

I literally want someone reading this to feel that spiritually. The pain you are feeling is all a part of the purpose for your life that's about to birth forth the plan of God. God led you to this book on purpose. Everything God spoke concerning you is already so because it is written in Numbers 23:19 that "God is not a man, that he should lie; Neither the son of man, that he should repent: Hath he said, and shall he not do it? Or hath he spoken, and shall he not make it good?" God specializes in taking everything that the enemy means for evil toward us and turning it around for our good. Where there is purpose, there will be pain; and the greater the purpose, the greater the pain. Our lives begin to make more sense when we grasp this concept and know all that the Word of God says concerning our going through different trials and tribulations we face in our lives.

Now after having my son, I had a made-up mind that I was done having children, but God had another plan. I had already told the doctor to do what he needed to do and got ready to sign papers, but they mentioned it in front of my ex-husband whom I never talked to about the decision. I just felt we already had so many things going wrong, we didn't need another child. But he heard the doctor, and he looked at me and said, in so many words, I was being selfish. I didn't even ask him if he wanted any more children. And I thought about what he said, and I felt bad about it, and I told the doctor, "That's okay. Don't do it."

He was being used to stop me from interrupting the plan of God. Well, after having my son, I got pregnant again. This time, I experienced something else I never experienced. Six weeks pregnant, but on certain days, I would feel this sharp pain that I thought was strange because I never had that happen before that early on. So we were headed to New Orleans, to his mother's house, and I wanted to help drive just a little. But while driving, that pain came again. It was happening more often, and when it would hit, I pressed my feet on the gas pedal more. Not intentionally, but the pain caused me to do it. And so he drove. But when we got to his mother's house, as I was sitting on the sofa, the pain hit again. So I went to lie down in one of the rooms at her house until we got ready to leave. We were headed to a room, and when we pulled up to the room, the pain hit in a way it never hit before, and this time, it didn't stop. I remember screaming so loud and crying really hard, and I couldn't even sit how I was sitting anymore. He asked If I thought I could make it inside. I shook my head and said no.

So he took me to the nearest hospital. It was so horrible. I didn't know what was going on, so the doctor did an internal ultrasound on me, and when he came back, he didn't have good news. I was lying on this bed. They had given me medicine for all that pain, but he drew on a piece of paper what was going on inside of me. He told me I had internal bleeding, in which I was bleeding inside of my body. He told me I had a tubal pregnancy and that the baby didn't go down the tube like a normal pregnancy, and it planted itself there. As the baby began to grow, this was why I felt the pain; and when it got too big for that small spot, it ruptured my tube. I had to go into immediate surgery, and he said that he would have to remove everything—the tubes and ovaries. He also told me that there was a possibility of death, that I could die during this surgery. Tears fell from my eyes as I signed the papers. I asked him if I could call my mom in Mississippi before going into surgery, and he said yes.

I remember calling my mother and telling her everything the doctor said to me, and she immediately started praying out very loud on the phone. She was praying in tongues (she prayed in the Spirit). I didn't know what she was saying, but she was praying to God, and I had to hang up the phone and was taken into surgery. Nobody could save me but God. My ex-husband couldn't help me. Nobody but God. I don't remember how long I was in surgery, but when I came out of surgery, I was in this room with lots of people, but my mom and brother were standing by my bed; I didn't even know they were coming from Mississippi to New Orleans, but the doctor came to me and told me something different from what he said before I went into surgery. He said that he was able to save everything on one side. He also told me and my ex-husband that it would be hard to have any more children. Well God had another plan because, a year later, I got pregnant again. This time, God allowed me to carry twins. I was like, "Okay, that's definitely enough." But these things were already spoken, and not only that, the day before my first ultrasound with the twins, I had a dream that I was buying two of everything, and then I said to my ex-husband, "If the doctor says it's two, I don't know what I'm going to do." And then I said, "Oh my" with laughter.

And I also told a friend of mine what I dreamed the day before. The next day, we went to the doctor, and I had an ultrasound. I still have pictures of that. She was showing us the baby, but the whole time, I was like there is something else there, and I never saw that with any of my other children, so she finally says, "Let me go get the doctor because it looks like twins." I looked at my ex-husband as he chuckled, and she was right, it was twins. When the doctor said it would be hard to have one child, God allowed me to carry two babies, and that was nothing but his plan and his purpose. It was meant for them to be here on the earth, and there was nothing we could do about it. We may have been lost, but our steps were still being ordered by the Lord, and that's nothing but the love of God. He was always so good to me, even in my foolishness, and he still is. I just love him, and I always tell people God is good all the time and, all the time, God is good. He allowed a lot of things to happen in my life, and he also chastised me when I needed it. He is a good father who knows all things, and I am just glad to be his daughter.

As you are reading this, I want to encourage you and tell you that your mistakes don't have to define your future. Jesus saves. I'm a living witness. My ex-husband and I went through all types of things that if God hadn't stepped in, somebody would have died. I've titled this book *Pained on Purpose*, as it was given to me, one night, by the Holy Spirit while I was on the phone with a friend of mine that I was coaching at the time. I've learned that in going through, it is like driving down a highway. The highways are made to lead us to different places in which we are going. Pain is just like that, and it serves a purpose. Its purpose is way bigger than anything that we may go through. As Paul was giving instructions to the church in Galatians 6:18, he wrote, "And let us not be weary in well doing: for in due season we shall reap, if we faint not." I love this because it's encouraging when going through hard times and dealing with the cares of this life. This part is what I call my spiritual journey in relation to the highway that I mentioned. It helped me to discover my God-given purpose on the earth.

I must start with my testimony of how God led me back to him. After running from him for so long, finally, at age thirty-three, God got my attention. It was a day like no other, but about three months prior to what I'm about to share, I cried out to God. I was alone at home this particular day, and I was drinking alcohol in the bathtub. My whole life began to flash before me, and I started crying out loud. I screamed out, "Why me, Lord? Why so much pain? Why did I have to go through all of that as a child?" I also remember saying to him, "Lord, I was only a child" again and again, and I kept screaming out loud so many things that I felt and wanted to know with tears falling from my eyes mixed with weeping. And when I got it all out, I yelled out one more time so loud, "Lord, help me! Please help me! I can't take this pain anymore!"

Somehow, after all of that, I fell asleep because I woke up hours later, and I was still in the bathtub. I managed to get myself together, and I went on about my day as usual, doing the usual things that I always did. About three months later, he answered my cry for help. There are some special days in life that we just never forget and, for me, it was a summer night, and I was headed out to party at a local club with a friend of mine. I had already planned to get wasted (drunk), so I parked my car close to home so I wouldn't have to drive far (as if that was safe). And she came to where I parked it and picked me up to ride with her because we both lived far from each other and far from the club. On our way there, we were having so much fun and doing exactly what was planned. When we pulled up to the club, we sat in the vehicle for a moment, just talking, laughing, drinking, and smoking. The only reason I remember the things I'm about to share is that she told me everything when we got back to work (we also worked together).

She told me that I took a drink out of my cup and said these exact words, "I'm tired of this, dawg" (dawg was our street way of saying homie or friend to each other). Then she said that I said,

"I don't care how drunk I get tonight. I'm going to church in the morning." And then I said, "Come on, let's have fun for the last time." The most amazing thing about that is that it really was the last time. There is a Bible scripture that says, "Death and life are in the power of the tongue" (Proverbs 18:21). And without knowing it, I was speaking life as well as calling those things that be not as though they were (Romans 8:17). Then we went inside the club and had an amazing time. I got so wasted that I don't even remember her bringing me back to my car, but she did. I do remember pulling in my driveway, though, because I had a flat tire out of nowhere, and it made so much noise, and the car started shaking really badly. After that, I don't remember anything else.

About 8:00 a.m. the next day, I was awakened by a hard push on the side of my body. It was so supernatural the touch from the push that I jumped up off the sofa that I was lying on, and I immediately turned my head to look at the time from the clock that was on my kitchen stove, and I instantly started looking for clothes to wear to church. And it was a battle going on spiritually because I kept hearing negative voices trying to talk me out of going in repeat in my head. I knew immediately that it was the voice of the enemy, but then I started thinking to myself that it must be something for me at this church for this voice to be so strong in my ear. But I kept trying to find something to wear and, finally, I got dressed, and I got ready to go to my car. But I forgot I had a flat tire, and I said to myself, "How am I going to get there?"

I was invited by my cousin to go to the church, and every time she asked me, I had a different excuse as to why I couldn't or wouldn't go. I also made a request unto God long before she invited me to go. I said, "Lord, I'll go if you show me that it's real and that you are there." I also did the same thing when I knew he was calling me back to him because, at that point, I knew that I was running from God. So I said to him, "Lord, if you ever want to get my attention, just make it very clear to me that it's you, and I will go." So I stood looking at the flat tire, and I thought about using my mother's vehicle, but I didn't know if she would let me use it because I had burned my bridges with her at that point in my life. But I took the chance anyway, and she was at her house at the time, and she was also battling cancer (and lost her eyesight). She went totally blind, and when I went into her room, I said, "Mom, can I use your car to go to church?"

She replied and said yes.

I was very surprised that she said yes but glad that she let me use it. She was probably shocked that I even asked. I had hardly any money to put gas in her vehicle. On top of that, I had a flat tire on my own car that I needed to get fixed, but I tried not to think about any of that because if I did, I knew that I wouldn't want to go to church. So I finally got myself together, and I left the house. I didn't know exactly where I was going, but I used the directions that my cousin texted to my cell phone. Now she wasn't there to help when I was going that day, and I couldn't reach her by phone, so I ended up at the wrong location at first to another church, but I didn't see any vehicles there, and I remember her telling me that the church had two services at the time, one in the morning and one in the afternoon. That's how I realized I was at a different church, so I left and continued down the other road, which led me directly to the church.

I saw a lot of cars and immediately got nervous, so much so that the palm of my hands started to sweat, and the voice came again, but even stronger this time. It was telling me not to go inside. It was a battle in the car between me and that voice. While battling in the car, the first services ended, and I saw the people coming out of the church. And there I was in the car, battling spiritually about going inside. But I decided to go inside for the second service. It was East Fernwood M. B. Church in McComb, Mississippi. When I walked in, one of the ushers greeted me with such a warm and welcoming smile which lifted me up and made me want to go on in even more, and I did. As soon as the choir started singing, I had flashbacks from my childhood of Mom bringing me to church.

I felt like I was at home, although I was in a strange land (place). I said that because I didn't know anybody there at the time, and my cousin who invited me wasn't there either. I sat at the very back on the last row in a corner, and when the preacher began to speak, I felt so bad, and I had my head down. The more he talked, the more I started crying (it was on a youth Sunday). And the youth pastor was speaking to us that day, and his message was titled "God Wants to Give You a Spiritual Makeover." Every word he spoke, I knew it was from God, and that's why the enemy did not want me to get there. But God had another plan. When he got to the end of his message, he asked those who could to stand up on their feet and close their eyes, and he said these words, "Ask yourself if you left out of these doors right today and lost your life, would God be pleased with you?"

I couldn't control the tears that were falling from my face, and I said to myself, "I'm not even pleased with myself." So I went quickly to the altar because God made it very clear to me that he was calling me, and right before the preacher prayed for all of us who came to the altar, he said these words, "When you go to do the same things you used to do, you won't be able to do them anymore."

And in my fleshly mind at the time, I said to myself, *Oh I heard that before*, but I kept crying out. And when he finished praying for us, we were led to the back of the church with other ministers who also spoke to us and wrote down the information that we gave to them so that they would be able to stay in contact with us, and the whole entire time, I was crying uncontrollably. I had no idea that my life was about to change in a major way, but it was what I had prayed for. The very next day, I tried to fall back into my old habits and way of living, but the more I tried to get into the flow of the old me, it just wasn't there anymore.

Everything was different this time, just like the preacher spoke that it would be at the altar, and I knew then that God had stepped in on my behalf. So I started to switch things up in my life, and I noticed the changes in me. I became so hungry for more of God and his Word. It was so strong I was running to Bible study and Sunday services, yearning to learn and hear more, and I found myself reading my Bible like a hungry person who hadn't eaten a meal in a very long time, and spiritually, that was me starving (me reading the Word and hearing the Word was feeding my spirit man). Jesus said in Matthew 4:4 that "man shall not live by bread alone, but by every word that proceedeth out of the mouth of God."

In other words, without the Word of God, we don't have life. We suffer spiritually, and we perish for the lack of knowledge (Hosea 4:6). I was cleaning my house and pausing to read on my breaks at work, reading, just making time to read any chance I got. I was falling asleep with my Bible in the bed, reading, waking up, just reading. I can't explain that type of hunger, and even now, I ask God to help me keep that same type of hunger because with time, it is so easy to pull back from it when we aren't pressing or pushing ourselves to do it. In Matthew 5:6, Jesus said to his disciples, "Blessed are they which do hunger and thirst after righteousness: for they shall be filled." I know that as time goes on and years begin to pass, in comparison, it's just like a natural relationship. We have to work even harder at the things that drew us to each other to keep the fire burning.

What I started noticing is that when I gave God a yes (by surrendering my life to him), he stepped in for me and my children in so many ways. He did so many supernatural things, and he taught me things while protecting us, and he is still doing that today. He is so awesome in all his ways. Giving him my life was the best choice I ever made. It didn't, and it still doesn't exclude any of us from hard times. In my experience, things got very hard, and it still does at times. But what I've also learned is that if we stay under God's umbrella (his wall of protection), he keeps us in ways we can't even imagine. He protects us from seen and unseen dangers.

I have also experienced times when I was just being hardheaded and how he always led me right back to him. It was only by his grace and his mercy that I wasn't consumed. It makes me so grateful and thankful for the undying love and affection that he has given to me. I don't know all of what the future holds, and I'm glad that he doesn't share everything with me because in this I've learned to walk more by faith and not by sight (2 Corinthians 5:7). Now before I begin to share him transitioning me into purpose, I just want to share a few of the testimonies of how he provided for me and my children when times got hard.

The first testimony is after the fire and the divorce and submitting my life back to God. I remember the food being very low, and I cooked the last meal that we had in the fridge and cabinets, and I tried to stretch that meal out until I got more groceries. And on the fourth day, the food started to smell so bad. As I am writing this, I have tears in my eyes, thinking back on that time because God has been so good to us, even then, but I said to myself and to God, "I can't feed this to my children." And I said, "God, you said in your Word that you would take care of us, and I am living for you the best that I know how." I said, "God, you are not a liar, and we need." At the time, I was doing home health (taking care of elderly clients at home), so I went to work that morning, and they were all at school. I went to one of the client's houses. While I was cleaning his house, I saw him in the kitchen, trying to close his freezer that was overflowing with food. He had so much that he couldn't close the door of the freezer. I never told him my situation, but he looked at me and asked me, "Could you use some of this food?"

I was so taken back that all I could do was say, "Yes," and I walked into his bathroom where I was cleaning, and I had a praise moment unto God. I started crying so hard and saying, "Thank you, Lord, for blessing us." I told him, "Thank you so much," and then I shared with him my situation before coming to his house. I was so amazed at how God touched his heart without even knowing my situation. It gave me so much hope, and I love sharing it with others, and I tell them that God will take care of his children and that he is a keeper of his Word. Faith is so powerful. When I prayed and talked to God, that was a faith move. And when I presented his Word back to him, that was faith being activated. In doing this, if he wouldn't have come through for us, then he wouldn't have kept his promised Word. And because he can't lie, he stepped in right on time.

Another particular time, I remember it being a very hot summer day, and we didn't have an air unit yet. I was so hot. I was in the kitchen trying to cook, and I was sweating so hard, and I looked at my children. The boys had taken off their shirts, trying to stay cool, and they were all fanning themselves with pieces of a cardboard box, and my oldest daughter's dad was on his way to our house to bring her some new clothes for school. And I did the same thing that I did with the food situation. I was in the kitchen, talking to God. I said, "Lord, I don't have the money to get an air unit, and it's so hot. I need you to help me." And we were in a double-wide trailer at the time, and it was pretty big and spacious inside, but I knew that if I had just one regular air conditioner in the window of one of the rooms that it would help to keep us cool until I could afford the unit.

Well, her dad showed up. He didn't come inside at first. He was talking to her and brought her the clothes. I was in the kitchen, and then I walked to the door where they were, and as he was getting ready to leave, I yelled out to him, "Hey! If you know anybody who has an air-conditioner, would you let me know?"

And he said, "Okay, I sure will."

I went back into the house, and I thought he had gotten in his car and left. But about five minutes later, I walked back by the front door, and I asked my daughter, "Why is your dad still parked outside, sitting in his car?"

She replied, "I don't know, Mama."

So I thought, *Well, maybe he is on his phone or something*, and I went back into the house, to the kitchen, then there was a knock on the door. Her dad never left the house, but he came back, and it was him knocking on the door. The children answered the door and called my name, so I walked into the living room, and he had put this box on the floor and, to my surprise, it was a brand-new air-conditioner. My eyes got so big, and I asked him, "Where did it come from?"

What he said next blew my mind even more. He said he just went to the store that same morning and purchased that one for his house 'cause he needed a new one but when while sitting in the car, he said to himself that we needed it more than he did, and he gave it to us. I was in a state of awe. I was thinking that even when he was sitting in his car, God touched his heart to give it to us. I cried and praised God all over again for being the awesome and amazing God that he is. He was growing me heavily in my faith, and I know that there is absolutely nothing that God can't do. The Bible says that he goes ahead of us and makes the crooked places straight. This is a great example and testimony that he keeps his Word. We went through so many different situations like these, and each time, it just made my faith grow stronger and stronger in the Lord.

One day, everything in the house we were living in at that time decided to break down. It started with the wiring, and it did something to the water, which made it stop flowing, and then the stove went out from a previous storm. It was all overwhelming. And when the water stopped flowing, I tried not to get frustrated. I was thinking to myself, *Really?* But before I could get any help, I told the kids that there was no water and all that was coming out of the kitchen sink was a very small drip, and I was thinking, *What am I going to do?* I placed a pot in the sink under the small drip of water that was coming out of the sink, not really thinking about it, and I just kept on doing what I needed to do at that moment. I continued, and I went into the bedroom and started folding clothes and completing other chores. When I walked back into the kitchen, to my surprise, the pot was filled with water. It seemed small, but it was a big matter for me. My children are my witnesses.

I started praising God right there in the kitchen. I was thanking God for the drip. The drip was so small. That's why I was so surprised. And then God revealed to me that everything he allowed us to go through wasn't just for me. His exact words were, "Lolita, the struggle isn't about you, but I am teaching your children how to survive as well as trust me in all situations." And because he is God who knows what is ahead of us, I know that he is preparing and has been preparing them also for their very own purposeful and personal future plans so that they will know that even when I am dead and gone, they can remember how to lean and depend on God. They have been taught through learning how to pray and through his Word and so much more. Proverbs 22:6 says, "Train up a child in the way he should go: And when he is old, he will not depart from it."

One of the greatest inheritances that we can leave our children with is to teach them about God, and I thank God for using my mother to teach me about him, even when I didn't want to hear it or go to church with her. She was only doing what the Word of God teaches us to do as parents and guardians. Romans 10:14 says, "How then shall they call on him in whom they have not believed? And how shall they believe in him of whom they have not heard? And how shall they hear without a preacher?" I had to learn in my own personal walk that, in spite of all the wrong that does go on in different churches and religions, the Word of God is still his words he left for us to guide us, and he wouldn't have had it written for us if it wasn't true.

In other words, there is still a remnant (a chosen people) that he has called to preach his Word that is teaching the truth and living it the best that they can in order to find that we have to seek God in prayer and let God lead and guide us in where to go. My advice to someone who is seeking God for a church to go to is to visit different places while you are seeking him in prayer about it until you feel or hear his Spirit saying this is where I want you to be. For me, the Word I was being taught at East Fernwood M. B. Church under the leadership of Pastor Jimmy J. Wilson/Evangelist Alisa Wilson, and many others, that God allowed him to use to teach us is what drew me in. The Word changed my life. I was doing what I was being taught, and I saw major changes and shifts for the better. The more I applied what I was being taught, the more I saw God move. And I knew from day one, I was in the place I was supposed to be. God used the youth pastor at the time to lead me back to him the first day I came there. Their names now are Pastor Cameron W. Jenkins and Minister Lukista Jenkins, and they are leaders of Opportunity Church in Gulfport, Mississippi.

Each and every one of them and many others shared the Word of God that helped me to grow, and I knew I couldn't leave the church in which God had placed me until God said that it was time to move, and that is what I did. I would encourage any believer to let God lead you, and if you are learning and growing by what you are being taught, then stay planted until God says otherwise. No matter the pain you may face, the betrayals, rejections, whatever you may face from the enemy, don't leave from under your God-given covering. The Holy Spirit will not lead you astray. So if he says, "Move," that means he already has a plan and a purpose in wherever he is taking you next.

These are just things I've learned in my own personal experiences in life. The Word of God is our map through life, and we need it to live. God will lead us in relationships, in ministry, in family matters, in business, and so much more through his Word. He led me to one of my careers by taking a regular job that I did not want to take. But in taking it, I found my passion for taking care of others, which led me to become a CNA (certified nursing assistant). I am still one now, fifteen years and counting. Now being called into ministry work and becoming an ordained evangelist, I never saw any of that in my future as a child or as an adult. I didn't even like school projects when we had to stand in front of the class and share what we did, let alone communicating with people and open and public speaking. And to be an effective witness for God, we must have a love for people in all, which I struggled with for many years after being hurt so many times in life. My heart turned and became cold. It never became a heart of hate, but it was an unhealed heart in which I put up a brick wall and blocked people out intentionally, out of the fear of being hurt again.

But being under the Word of God, God revealed to me that he had more for me to do for him and that I couldn't take these issues with me. He told me that I had to deal with them, and once he revealed that clearly to me, I asked him to teach me how to love again. Having the heart to please God, I started seeking him about my purpose. I was praying and asking him what he created me to do on the earth. Well, after praying and seeking for so long, one day, while in Bible study, my pastor at the time had a prayer line, and almost everyone in church was in the line, waiting to receive prayer. While I was sitting, I heard the Spirit say to me, "Go get in the line for prayer, and your pastor is going to tell you your purpose."

I didn't tell anyone what I heard. I just obeyed the voice of God and got in the line. When it was my time for prayer, I stood before him with lifted hands. He turned around away from me and looked at the musicians, and he asked them to play a different music, and they did. I didn't know what was about to happen, and he continued to talk to them for a few minutes, then he turned around toward me. He never touched me or anything. He just spoke one word, and he said, "Prophetess" and, immediately, the Spirit touched me so heavily. I began to spin around very fast. I remember I was trying to use all of my strength to stop myself from spinning. But the power of God was too powerful, and he was speaking about many other things that have all come to pass in my life, including traveling to other countries. And when I came out of the spin, I was on another side of the church, just looking at my pastor, thinking to myself, *How did he tell me exactly what I heard God say that he would say to me when I get in the prayer line?* I was amazed. When he spoke, I believe there was an impartation and a spiritual awakening that took place inside of me that was transferred by the Holy Ghost through my pastor.

And the very first time that God used me to speak publicly, I was in a spiritual battle. All the doubt, insecurities, and so much more came over me. I said to God, "I can't do that. I'm not smart enough. I don't know how to, and I don't want to let you down, and I've never spoken in front of people before." The battle was so strong that I fell asleep with the Bible on my chest, talking to God. He then led me to Moses in the Bible.

After reading his Word, he said to me, "You are exactly how I want you to be, totally depending upon me so that I, your God, may be glorified." And I cried, and I asked him to help me. I called my pastor and talked to him about everything because I was in a battle, and he told me that God wanted me to do it. Then he told me to fast and pray, and he gave me specific instructions even more on how to seek God. And I obeyed his voice and did everything he told me to do. After doing that, God spoke to me in a dream and gave me everything he wanted me to share with the people. God wasn't telling me just to do that, but he was showing me what he had placed inside of me. Once God spoke those words through my pastor, I started seeking God even more about what work he wanted me to do in the kingdom of God. And I also made a request to God myself. I asked him to send me where nobody wants to go. And after praying that prayer, he placed me in "Outreach over the Women's Prison Ministry" and in teaching the youth.

I've always been hurt, rejected, neglected, and felt so low in my life that it made me have a strong passion for others who are going through the same things that I went through and more. To all of you that are reading this right now, I want to tell you that there is always an assignment attached to our purpose. Whatever your purpose may be, God has a reason that he has placed you in that position or will place you in a position for his work to be done through you to help somebody else. One thing I've learned is that whatever purpose is being fulfilled, you'll feel so alive inside while doing it. I'm not saying it will be easy, and some days you may want to quit, but God will give you all you need to carry on.

He will be your peace, he will be your guide, he will be your strength, and he will protect and provide. When I got into my career in taking care of the elderly, I knew I was doing what I was called to do, especially now more than ever (because I am able to witness to my clients while taking care of them all at the same time). I could have quit when I started because of the pay, and the first time, a resident died, and they told me and my coworkers that we had to wash his body for the funeral home to come get him. I went to my car and thought about quitting then, but my spirit man told me to go back inside, and I did because my passion for it was greater than the money and what I had to deal with. And because I stuck with it in unfavorable times, God has tripled the pay. You see, if God has given you a vision work it, even when the odds are stacked against you. If it is his purpose for you, know that he will reward your faithfulness to it. God is so amazing. He will always equip us with what we need to accomplish what he wants us to achieve.

Now to those of you who have a prophetic gift, you will experience a different type of walk as many others. But I'm speaking on this at the moment from my own experiences. Even as a child, the things I saw that came to pass were sometimes painful and overwhelming. One of the hardest for me was seeing people die, especially those I knew and was close to me, including my very own mother and clients that I took care of in my adult life. Also having to share things that I didn't really want to share but knowing that if I didn't obey God, I myself would suffer the consequences. I learned all of this and more the hard way. But once I learned that God equips us for the perfecting of the saints, for the work of the ministry, and for the edifying of the body of Christ, it was easier for me to submit to the will of God and the call, which he placed over my life. You can read more about that directly out of the Bible in Ephesians 4:11–12.

I have so many supernatural experiences and testimonies that I will also share as I am led in future books to come or however God leads me to share them. I will say this, though. Sometimes our purpose can lead us to transition from one place to another. Transitioning isn't always easy either because you have to know without a shadow of a doubt that you heard God. Once you know that God is transitioning you, depending on your situation, for me, it was being transitioned into another state. He made it so clear to me, and I was praying a lot and seeking him during that time because of what he was already showing and speaking to me. He showed it in dreams to me and my oldest daughter. He spoke it through my leader and other leaders during the time I was praying. I never told any of them that I was praying and seeking God about it, and I only started seeking him because of what I was seeing, hearing, and feeling in my spirit.

After God made it clear to me, I still wanted to talk to my leader (my pastor) because it was something major to me, and I felt that talking to someone who has been through it before would help me a whole lot, and I did. What was even more confirmation is we had scheduled to talk and meet after Bible study one Wednesday night. I didn't tell him what I wanted to talk about in detail before Bible study that day. I just told him I needed to talk to him about something that was heavy on my heart. Well, him being led by the Spirit, he came into the sanctuary to teach us that night, but he came in singing a song, and he started to sing, "Time is filled with swift transitions," and I started crying so hard because I already knew that God was getting ready to shift my location.

It was hard because I didn't want to leave my church family, but I also didn't want to disobey God. So we talked afterward, and he confirmed even more what I already knew. But it wasn't until I got to the next destination that I realized why God moved me, especially on the job and the people I've met from day to day. Taking care of people, as I've mentioned, is a ministry all by itself. I've had to minister to people on their deathbeds. I've had to pray for them and encourage them and family members and friends as well as lead some to give their lives to Christ, and they did. God always has a plan bigger than what we can see or comprehend; he just wants us to be willing and obedient, and even with my church family here in the state of Pennsylvania, God is growing me even deeper in the area of love and other ways as well. But love was something that was snatched away from me at an early age by the enemy as well as my identity and character and so much more. And I am grateful that it all happened now, though. You see, even while we are walking out our purpose and doing the will of God, he will forever be our number one teacher (growing us, maturing us, cleaning us, shaping us, making us, and molding us into who he has created us to be). The best thing we can do is surrender our lives and our will over to him so that he can have his own way in our lives and also through us.

John 3:16 says: "For God so loved the world, that he gave his only begotten Son, that whosoever believeth in him should not perish, but have everlasting life." Romans 10:9 also says: "That if you confess with your mouth the Lord Jesus, and shall believe in your heart that God hath raised him from the dead, you shall be saved." Although my story and your story are still being written, as long as we are living on this earth, we must continue to walk by faith and not by sight. God is in total control, and your pain serves a God-given purpose. Pain brings eternal gain. We must go through to get to where God wants us to be. Know this: that there is nothing wrong with you because you have it hard or have had a rough life as I did, you are just *Pained on Purpose*.

This book I have written, as I have been led and inspired by the Holy Spirit, to help others who may have experienced a lot of different pain and heartaches in life. I share a lot of personal testimonies and things that I've faced and overcame because of Jesus Christ and those he used along the way to help me. My purpose in writing this is that someone will be drawn to God and that they would want to turn their lives over to him and let him help them, just as he has helped me and many others. I didn't want to leave this earth without sharing my story with as many people as I can so that they can see and know that there is hope and purpose after all the heartache and pain.

God can restore, and he is a healer and a deliverer; meaning, there is nothing that we do that he can't save us from no matter how bad it is. I pray that you are inspired and uplifted after reading this book. I am the author, Lolita A. Baker. I am also a certified life and health coach for anyone who wants or needs coaching. You can book appointments through my website at www.ggsresources.com. I am also a certified nursing assistant, evangelist, and mother of four children. There are so many people that I did not mention by name who have been a great blessing to me and my family along the way, and I want to personally thank each and every one of you. But, most importantly, I thank God for being a keeper of his Word. God bless you all.

ABOUT THE AUTHOR

Lolita A. Baker is a certified life and health coach and a business owner of GG's Resources where her online coaching services are offered and found at www.ggsresources.com. She is also a certified nursing assistant for over fifteen years now, a mother of four wonderful children, and an ordained evangelist.

Online coaching services are offered & found at www.ggsresources.com.